Dance

HIP-HOP AND URBAN DANCE

Tamsin Fitzgerald

Heinemann Library
Chicago, Illinois

Customer Service 888-454-2279
Visit our website at www.heinemannlibrary.com

Editorial: Sarah Shannon and Robyn Hardyman
Design: Steve Mead and Geoff Ward
Illustration: Sarah Kelly
Picture Research: Maria Joannou
Production: Duncan Gilbert

Originated by Modern Age
Printed and bound by Leo Paper Group

13 12 11 10 09
10 9 8 7 6 5 4 3 2 1

Library of Congress Cataloging-in-Publication Data
Fitzgerald, Tamsin, 1950-
  Hip-hop and urban dance / Tamsin Fitzgerald.
     p. cm. -- (Dance)
  Includes bibliographical references and index.
  ISBN 978-1-4329-1378-6 (hc)
  1. Hip-hop dance--Juvenile literature. I. Title.
  GV1796.H57F58 2008
  793.3--dc22
                        2008016092

Acknowledgments
The publishers would like to thank the following for permission to reproduce photographs:
© Alamy Images pp. 17 (Music Stock), 20 (Philipp Hympendahl), 41 (Andrea Matone); © Bill Mohn p. 39, © Camera Press p. 35 (Grant Scott); © Corbis pp. 4 (Reuters/Claro Cortes), 5, 29 (Bettmann), 13, 26, 32 (Danser/Nicolas Six), 19 (HSI Productions/ZUMA i); © Getty Images pp. 10 (Frank Micelotta), 18 (Matthew Simmons), 27 (Scott Gries), 30 (Jon Furniss/WireImage), 31 (Dave Hogan), 33 (China Pictures), 40 (Joe Raedle); © PA Photos p. 36 (Empics/Alma Robinson); PYMCA p. 7 (Leonard Smith); © Redferns p. 9 (Paul Bergen); © Rex Features pp. 14-15, 16 (Everett Collection/CSU Archives), 23 (Sipa Pres), 25 (Alex Sudea), 34, 38, 43 (Alastair Muir); © Wayne Simmonds p. 37.

Cover photograph of break dancing reproduced with permission of © Getty Images/Digital Vision.

CONTENTS

Some words are printed in bold, **like this.** You can find out what they mean by looking in the glossary, on page 46.

STREET CULTURE

We see it in movies, on TV in advertisements and music videos, and in the theater. What are we talking about? Hip-hop, or urban dance. Hip-hop dance has not been around for very long, but in the last 10 years it has flung itself into our living rooms, onto our movie screens, into our schools, and onto our stages. But what is hip-hop?

Street culture

Hip-hop is a lifestyle. It is based on unique new art forms that developed on the streets out of a need for self-expression. It is commonly thought to contain four elements: **DJ-ing**, **MC-ing**, **graffiti**, and **b-boying** (break dancing).

How did hip-hop begin? Who are the past and future pioneers of this exciting dance style? How do you go about learning this style, and what place does it have in the future of dance and the theater? For the history we need to look at the music, the art, the people, and, of course, the streets.

▶ B-boys hit their moves on the streets as crowds gaze on in amazement.

An era of change

During the 1960s, the United States experienced a lot of social and economic changes. It was a time of great unrest, including protests against the Vietnam War, and young Americans began to question the power of the government and of big corporations. This atmosphere helped the growing civil rights movement, which demanded full rights for African Americans.

The social unrest of the 1960s was expressed in popular music by musicians such as the Beatles, Jimi Hendrix, and Bob Dylan. The dance world was going through a time of experimentation, rejecting trained dancers, traditional sets, and costumes for a more basic look and feel. Social dances such as the Twist, Mashed Potato, and Locomotion took hold of the teenage population.

The birth of hip-hop

In the **Bronx** district of New York City, poverty was widespread, gangs were everywhere, and crime was on the increase. Young people were looking for a means of self-expression and a way to create a sense of identity. They began to experiment with music, dance, art, and speech. Out of this experimentation, out of the Bronx, grew hip-hop.

Biography

Earl Tucker
Some of the origins of hip-hop dance are credited to a dancer named Earl Tucker, known as "snake hips." Tucker performed in **Harlem** music clubs in the 1920s and early 1930s, and his moves are considered similar to some early break dance moves.

▼ These protestors are demonstrating against the Vietnam War in Washington, D.C., in 1969.

FOUR ELEMENTS OF HIP-HOP

Out of the unrest in the United States, and the self-expression and experimentation of the young, came the four elements of hip-hop: **b-boying** (break dancing), **DJ-ing**, **MC-ing** (rapping), and **graffiti**. These four elements paved the way for a wave of amazing new artists who catapulted hip-hop culture across the globe. The artists turned b-boying into what we know today as one of the main urban dance styles.

Dance facts

Hip-hop culture
KRS-One, a legend in the hip-hop world who formed Boogie Down Productions and has released classics such as "Criminal Minded," believes there are nine elements to hip-hop. These are the original four plus **beatboxing**, hip-hop fashion, hip-hop slang, **street knowledge**, and **street entrepreneurship**.

B-boying

B-boying, or breaking, is the dancing—or physical expression—of hip-hop. B-boying began on the streets with little more than a "boom box" (a large portable sound system) and a piece of cardboard to spin on. B-boying is about a lifestyle that involves dedication and passion. It is about style, dancing, battling, power, and families. It began with James Brown, Afrika Bambaata, and the Rock Steady **Crew** and is now one of the fastest-growing and most evolving styles of dance.

DJ-ing

DJ-ing is the musical expression of hip-hop. It involves using turntables, records, mixers, and **scratching**. The first person to use these techniques was DJ Kool Herc. He used twin turntables to cut back and forth between tracks, and also extended the instrumental sections (that dancers would dance to) to create a new sound known as the "**break**." It was called this because there was a break from the **lyrics**. DJ-ing is now a huge industry. What DJs do is sometimes called "**turntablism**," and the DJs are sometimes called "turntablists." They scratch, mix records, and compete to win titles in the same way as those involved in the other elements of hip-hop.

▲ Graffiti artists demonstrate their skill on New York subway cars.

MC-ing

MC-ing, or rapping, as it became known, is the verbal expression of hip-hop. It involves speaking to the beat of the music using rhyme. It may relate to a theme or send out an important message. Kool Herc and the Herculoids were the first to MC, and since then MC-ing has developed into a huge industry. Competitions take place all over the world.

Graffiti

Graffiti is the visual expression of hip-hop. It began in the 1960s when a well-known graffiti artist, Taki 183, regularly marked the New York subway with his "tag" (identification). Soon, many young people were "graffing" whole sides of trains with messages, names, and art. This is depicted in the movie *Style Wars* (1983). It is important to know that graffiti is illegal. If caught, graffiti artists can face arrest for vandalism (destroying or defacing public property). Famous graffiti artists such as Banksy have won awards for their work, but their faces remain secret so that they are not arrested.

B-BOYING AND CREWS

When we think of **b-boying**, or break dancing, we think of **head spins**, **windmills**, the **worm**, **freezes**, and general displays of gravity-defying movement. B-boying has not always been this way.

In the late 1960s in New York, poverty was widespread, fighting and gangs were commonplace, and there were "turf wars" (fights to claim territory) between rivals. The Black Spades were one of the biggest and toughest gangs in New York at the time. Young people in the **Bronx** were looking for a voice and a way to prove they had a future.

The godfather of soul

At this time, the performer James Brown, who was known as "the godfather of soul," was gaining popularity. His dancing style involved fast and **raw** movements such as spins, quick shuffles, knee drops, and the splits. A craze soon followed called the "Good Foot," named after his hit "Get on the Good Foot." This was later renamed "The B-Boy." It involved high-energy dance moves, and it formed a framework for b-boying.

Biography

B-boys of the 1970s

The first wave of b-boys included the Zulu Kings, Klark Kent, the Amazing Bobo, and Jon Sizzle. The second wave included Jimmy J, Phase 2, and Melle Mel. The third wave included Ken Swift, Frosty Freeze, and Crazy Legs.

The godfather of hip-hop

Some young people and gangs in the Bronx started b-boying. B-boys in different gangs started battling with their moves instead of their weapons. This form of battle was called **up rock**, and it involved no physical contact. Up rock gave way to other dance moves such as **down rock** or **floor rock**. This was b-boying in its earliest form, with none of the power moves we see today.

In 1969 hip-hop musician Afrika Bambaataa founded Zulu Nation, an "international hip-hop awareness group." As b-boying emerged, he decided that it could lead to something positive for a lot of gang members, and he encouraged young people to keep dancing. He set up one of the first b-boy **crews**, the Zulu Kings. The Zulu Kings were made up of local Bronx kids who would perform at talent shows and in clubs. They quickly gained respect and popularity.

▼ Respected hip-hop legend Afrika Bambaataa spins his tunes.

This first wave of b-boy popularity lasted until 1977. Afrika Bambaataa encouraged change and gave hope to many. He saw that gang violence was reduced as a result of the rise of hip-hop.

Crews

A crew is a group of individual b-boys or b-girls who have come together. They see themselves as a family. Each crew has a unique style but one common purpose—to be the best. The members do this by competing and being crowned champions. A crew can have many members, but it normally competes using between six and ten members.

▲ These original members of the Rock Steady Crew demonstrate their moves at the VH1 Hip-Hop Honors awards show in 2004.

The Rock Steady Crew

In 1977 two Bronx b-boys, Jimmy D and Jojo, established a crew called the Rock Steady Crew. To get into the Rock Steady Crew, people had to be the best b-boys, battling to win their place. However, by this stage, the craze of b-boying had died down and the Freak, another dance style, was the new fad.

It was not until 1981 that things began really to take off for the Rock Steady Crew. The photographer and sculptor Henry Chalfant offered the crew a chance to perform at the Lincoln Center Outdoors Program, in New York. The performance was also a battle with rival b-boys from the Dynamic Rockers. It was covered by local television stations, as well as by publications including the *New York Times*, the *Village Voice*, the *Daily News*, and *National Geographic*. The performance was a turning point in hip-hop history, because it took the style to a much wider audience. Jimmy D took notice of the craze that had started in Manhattan. He made three influential members of the crew—Crazy Legs, Frosty Freeze, and Ken Swift—into president and co-vice presidents of the Rock Steady Crew.

The Rock Steady Crew performed at the Ritz nightclub alongside Afrika Bambaataa, the Jazzy 5, and a punk rock group called Bow Wow Wow. After their performance, Crazy Legs and Frosty Freeze asked Afrika Bambaataa if they could be part of the Zulu Kings, the most highly respected of all b-boy crews. Afrika Bambaataa allowed not only them but also the entire Rock Steady Crew to become members of the Zulu Kings. He knew that they would play an important role in spreading the peaceful message of Zulu Nation.

Amazing fact

Royal invitation

The Rock Steady Crew had major success performing all over the world. In 1983 the crew was asked by the queen of England to perform at the Royal Variety Performance in London. During this time, Charisma Records approached them with a record deal. Their record "Hey You, The Rock Steady Crew" reached number 38 on the U.S. charts. It did much better in the United Kingdom, soaring to the top 10 and selling over one million copies.

Breaking

In the 1980s, the media started to call b-boys and b-girls "breakers" or "break dancers." The phrase "break dance" is now widely used to describe the dancing, but it is not considered to be a true hip-hop phrase, and dancers working within hip-hop would still describe themselves as b-boys or b-girls.

Breaking boundaries

B-boying has developed in many ways over the years. With b-boys pushing their bodies to extremes, breaking is now even more daring. As b-boys work to add an extra spin, **flare**, or hop to outdo their competitors, the boundaries are constantly being broken.

Head spins involve b-boys spinning on their heads, using their legs to control or increase the number of spins. From some of the basic freezes, such as a shoulder freeze, b-boys have searched for smaller body parts to balance on. Innovations include balancing on two hands to the forearm, one hand, elbow, and even the knuckles, and being upside down, sideways, inverted, or turning.

Dance facts

Korea's relationship with b-boys

B-boying in South Korea has grown into a massive cultural phenomenon. In 2002 Korean b-boy crew Expression won the Battle of the Year title in Germany. They were followed in 2004 and 2005 by Korean crews Gambler and Last for One. This winning streak gave the crews international respect and recognition, and the city government of Seoul, its tourism board, and commercial sponsors started to fund Korean B-boys. B-boys in Korea are used to promote the country and its culture, in the same way that music or movie stars are in the United States. The Korean capital, Seoul, even has its own b-boy theater, where b-boy shows are performed all year round.

French crew Pokemon, winner of many b-boy battles, performs its routine.

Across the globe

Breaking is a worldwide phenomenon, with crews and soloists from across the globe competing to be crowned champions. The French crews Vagabond and Pokemon are two of the best. Vagabond was the Battle of the Year Champion in 2006, and Pokemon won the World Crew Title at the 2006 UK B-Boy Championships. Other crews to watch out for are the Korean crews Extreme and Expression, the British crew Soul Mavericks, and the Japanese crew Mortal Combat.

Biography

Tip Crew
Tip Crew from Korea won the crew element of the Sony Ericsson B-Boy Championships in 2007. Korea produces some of the world's most extreme dancers, with the most daring moves.

B-GIRLS FIGHT BACK

B-girls have the same history as b-boys, but it has taken longer for the girls to establish themselves in the world of hip-hop. B-girls have often found themselves on the edge of a b-boy **crew**. Due to the power and strength needed for some of the breaking moves, in the past b-girls often found themselves sidelined, left to do footwork and some basic **freezes**.

▼ B-girls strut their stuff at the 3rd annual World Hip-Hop Championships in 2004.

Today, though, b-girls are fighting back and firmly establishing themselves within the b-boy scene. With their own crews, competitions, and festivals, b-girls have now firmly found their place in the male-dominated world of hip-hop and have been given the respect they deserve.

Best b-girls

Asia One from the United States has long been known not only as one of the best b-girls but also as a businesswoman, because she promotes hip-hop on a global scale. As the creator of the annual B-Boy Summit, an international four-day conference for b-boys and b-girls, Asia One has gained respect and recognition for her work worldwide. British b-girl Hanifa Macqueen-Hudson, formally known as "Bubbles," rose to fame in the 1980s. Other top b-girls and crews making their mark on a global scale are Rokafella from the **Bronx** (U.S), Firefly (United Kingdom), Dirty Mamas (Germany), Shebang Crew (Canada), Female Artistics (Austria), Da Ladie Breakers (Hong Kong), and No Easy Props (U.S.).

Dance facts

B-boy and b-girl words
"bite"—steal a move
"sick"—really good
"wack"—not very good
"heavy"—amazing
"props"—respect

FUNK STYLES

Funk styles form a collection of street dance styles that fall under the umbrella of hip-hop dance.

Locking

Locking is a style of street dance that features strong arm and hand movements with relaxed hips. Wrist rolls, bounces, pauses, and points make up some of the movements, along with a bold performance style. It is funky, fast, and full of synchronized moves that were originally performed to funk music.

In 1969 in Los Angeles, California, a street dancer named Don Campbell was doing a new dance style that he called the "Campbellock." He formed his own company of dancers called the Lockers. The Lockers had a very distinctive style. They wore bright, colorful shirts, striped socks, cropped pants, bow ties, white gloves, platform shoes, and hats. The Lockers would move using both **choreographed** routines and through **improvising**. For the improvised sections, they would stand in a line, with some taking

▶ The hit TV show *Soul Train* started in 1971. It featured R&B, soul and hip-hop artists, helping make the latest fashions and dance trends popular.

turns to step forward, make up moves on the spot, and then step back. As the Lockers became more famous, they made appearances on the hit TV program *Soul Train*. This helped to make locking more popular.

The robot

At around the same time locking was developing, another new style of funk dance was beginning to make waves among dancers. The hit TV show *Lost in Space* inspired dancers like Charles Washington to do a dance called the robot. The robot is a style of movement in which dancers imitate a robot by contracting and releasing their muscles to make the robot move. The robot dance caught on quickly, but was later popularized even more by Michael Jackson in his moonwalk. The moonwalk gives the illusion that the dancer is walking forward, while he or she is actually moving backward.

Boogaloo

In Fresno, California, a dancer named Sam Solomon (Boogaloo Sam) was inspired by both Charles Washington and the Lockers. He invented a new style called Boogaloo, named after James Brown's song "Do the Boogaloo." Boogaloo took its influences from both the robot and locking. Boogaloo uses every part of the body and includes rolling the hips, knees, and head.

In 1977 Boogaloo Sam formed a group called the Electronic Boogaloo Lockers. Later they were renamed the Electric Boogaloos. The Electric Boogaloos are still dancing today, teaching and keeping the "funk" alive.

Technique

Popping
Popping involves contracting and relaxing muscles to create a popping effect, normally known as a hit or pop. Some other funk styles include floating, strobing, tutting, puppet, scarecrow, waving, and ticking.

▲ The originators of funk, the Electric Boogaloos, perform on stage at the Breaking Convention in 2007.

NEW DEVELOPMENTS

With **b-boying**, **locking**, **popping**, and other street dance styles firmly established in hip-hop culture, it was inevitable that new moves and styles would appear on the scene. As hip-hop dance continues to develop and evolve, other influences are finding their way into this world. The term "urban dance" is now commonly used to describe these.

Clowning and krumping

In 1992 Tommy the Clown entered the arena, and a new style of urban dance and clowning was created. Clowning involved dancing at children's birthday parties, dressed as a clown, doing a mixture of street dance moves. Tommy realized that he could offer young people an alternative to gangs, drugs, and violence through creativity and expression. He created a following of hip-hop clowns. In his academy the word "krump" was used to describe the intensity of a dance move, and **krumping** was born. Since then clowning has grown into a global phenomenon, with performances worldwide.

In 2005 a movie documentary *Rize* was created by award-winning director and photographer David LaChapelle. *Rize* introduced the world to a new form of hip-hop dance that involved the use of brightly colored costumes and makeup.

▶ Tommy the Clown performs to the camera at the Rock This Way tour in Hollywood 2005.

▲ These dancers from the movie *Rize* are demonstrating their krumping moves.

Spiritual warfare

Krumping is different from clowning. It does not involve wearing makeup or a costume and is highly energetic. It is sometimes called spiritual warfare. It involves movements such as chest pops (the thrusting of the chest in and out), stomps, and arm swings. Krumping is a progression of clowning and is growing in popularity all the time.

In addition to the new waves of clowning and krumping, there are also other forms of urban dance appearing in studios across the globe. Some of these include house, funk, street jazz, new wave hip-hop, and street flava.

Technique

Krump moves

"flashy"—quick foot movements and sharp, precise, showy moves

"goofy"—the least aggressive of the krump styles, usually funny and energetic (pioneered by the krump practitioner Goofy)

"jerk"—motions that are not smooth and flowing but still artistic

"rugged"—fewer tricks; more of a pure essence

"technical"—mix of flashy and smooth; a crowd-pleasing style

Parkour

Parkour, or free running, was created by a French performer named David Belle. It is a way of traveling across obstacles to reach a destination. Belle describes it as "like being chased across an urban landscape and having to get over obstacles in the most effcient way possible." It is daring, graceful, and athletic, and it contains movements from diverse disciplines such as gymnastics, climbing, martial arts, and acrobatics.

Parkour is becoming increasingly popular. In the same way that the world became aware of break dance, parkour is finding its way into commercials, music videos, movies, and onto the stage. Like b-boying, it has begun to make its way from the streets into theaters.

▼ A young parkour **crew** flies through the air, demonstrating the danger and beauty of this recent urban art form.

It is the athletic combination of bird-like movement, heart-stopping acrobatics, spins, and jumps mixed with vertigo-inducing fear that makes parkour so exhilarating. In a recent production called *Traces* by a French-Canadian circus/dance troupe called 7 Fingers, elements of parkour could be seen as an acrobat jumped and flew between two poles.

New combined with old

Other influences that have found their way into the world of urban dance are from other urban art forms and sports such as basketball, skateboarding, tap, and circus skills. Yet, like basic ballet technique, b-boying has some fundamental steps that remain untouched and pure. A six-step (in which dancers' feet move in six steps around their hands) will always be a six-step, even if the style in which it is performed by the b-boy or b-girl varies.

Urban dance is not alone when it comes to using other influences. Ballet and contemporary dance have long borrowed styles from each other, and influences from hip-hop are now making their way into modern dance.

Step 1
Step 2
Step 3
Step 4
Step 5
Step 6

◀ This movement is the Six Step, an essential movement for anyone learning hip-hop.

HIP-HOP DANCE AND MUSIC

Hip-hop dance and music have always gone hand in hand. It was the innovation of the music that inspired the dance style of **b-boying**. The two follow each other closely, and the music that is played while b-boys and b-girls move is very important. It can set the pace, dynamics, move, and style of the dance. The tracks chosen by the DJs, the way the music is mixed, the **break** in the music, and the **lyrics** can all determine whether or not the track becomes popular. There are many artists today who have echoes of hip-hop in their music, such as Justin Timberlake and Rihanna, but they are not hip-hop artists in the true sense of the word. For many, hip-hop is a way of life and not something that can be added to sell a record.

The 1960s and 1970s

As we have seen, hip-hop music originated in the **Bronx** in the late 1960s and early 1970s. At parties, DJs would separate the percussion sections between the verses in songs to create an extended "break" in the music. DJ Kool Herc is one of the originators of hip-hop music. Using funk, soul, and disco music, Herc started using an audio mixer and two records. This allowed him to mix two records together. Not long after this, Grand Wizard Theodore invented **scratching**, the art of moving the record back and forth under the needle in a rhythmic fashion.

At these parties, people would keep the partygoers entertained in between songs. They would introduce the tunes, excite the crowds, and entertain. They became known as MCs. ("MC" stands for "Master of Ceremonies.") The first MC **crew** was Kool Herc and the Herculoids. From **MC-ing** came rap. MCs began rhyming what they were saying, **improvising** on the spot. Rappers, on the other hand, learned their lyrics beforehand and generally would rap about their lives, themselves, or important social or political topics. Some of the first rap records were Grandmaster Flash's

"Super Rappin" and the Sugarhill Gang's "Rapper's Delight." This type of hip-hop became known as East Coast hip-hop because it originated in New York, on the east coast of the United States.

The 1980s

By the 1980s, hip-hop was really popular. New artists such as LL Cool J, Kurtis Blow, and Run DMC released records that hit the mainstream charts. Collaborating with the rock group Aerosmith, hip-hop artists Run DMC had global success with "Walk this Way." Female hip-hop duo Salt-N-Pepa also arrived on the scene in 1985. They were the first black female group to have success, with tracks such as "The Show Stoppa" and "Push It."

▲ Female hip-hop duo Salt-N-Pepa, here in 1994, rapped and danced their way to worldwide success.

West Coast hip-hop

West Coast hip-hop exploded onto the scene in the late 1980s, with artists such as Dr. Dre, Ice T, Snoop Doggy Dog, and Tupac Shakur. It is more commonly known as gangsta rap. This type of hip-hop was more melodic, but the lyrics were often controversial, creating an image that brought publicity but also problems. The abusive content of the lyrics was perceived by some as promoting violence, racism, sexism, and **homophobia**. Some gangsta rappers disagree with this, saying that the lyrics just represent the struggles of their inner-city lives.

Electro

Another style of music to come out of the early hip-hop scene was electro (or electro funk). Body **poppers** often choose to dance to electro. This is because it contains electronic sounds, has a strong beat with a natural pop or hit, and the vocals are sometimes robotic and distorted electronically. Afrika Bambaataa's "Planet Rock" was one of the first electro records. It was followed by Hashim's "Al-Naafiysh" ("The Soul").

Dance facts

Turntablist competitions
When turntablists compete, they each perform a routine—a combination of various technical scratches, beat juggles (changing a sample), and other elements including body tricks (using various body parts such as the elbow, chin, back, and even nose to mix and scratch records). Invisibl Skratch Piklz is one of the best turntablist crews. It consists of U.S. and Filipino DJs.

Other musical influences

Hip-hop music, like hip-hop dance, has always used outside influences. Whether it uses rock, metal, or house, it is constantly changing and progressing. Hip-hop is now a huge global business, with new artists creating new sounds all over the world. Artists, the music they produce, and the dance performed to this music in videos and on TV shows influence what we perceive to be popular or fashionable. A lot of the time the dance styles we are seeing relate more to jazz dance than to hip-hop dance, however.

In the same way that b-boying has a competitive nature, so does hip-hop music, with competitions in MC-ing, rapping, **turntablism**, and **beatboxing.**

Dance facts

Human beatbox

The term "beatbox" was used as slang for drum machines produced in the late 1970s that could not be programmed. When people could not afford to buy these, they used their mouth instead to create the beats. In the 1980s, there were three pioneers of this art form: Darren "Buffy" Robinson, Doug E. Fresh, and Biz Markie. In the late 1990s, artists such as Killa Kela and Rahzel pushed beatboxing to new levels. They added new music styles such as **drum 'n' bass** and introduced vocal scratching as well as singing and beating at the same time.

▲ Beatboxer Killa Kela drops some beats at a performance in 2007.

HIP-HOP AND CLOTHING

When we think of hip-hop or urban dance, we think of baseball caps, baggy pants, oversized T-shirts, bandannas, and, of course, the all-important sneakers. Hip-hop dancers tend to wear baggy clothes that are comfortable to dance in. This is less true of commercial hip-hop, however. On TV shows and in hip-hop videos, women often wear very little clothing, typically bikini tops and hot pants.

▲ B-boys show off their moves while looking cool in baggy clothes and baseball caps. They wear knee pads on their elbows for protection.

Essential hip-hop fashions

Image and hip-hop run side by side, and the clothing worn often makes a statement about the person who is dancing. There are few official rules on the clothing, but there are several essential items:

- Baseball cap: Used by b-boys to protect their heads when **head spinning** and often used as a prop in routines
- Knee pads: Worn by urban dancers under their pants to protect their knees and also sometimes worn to protect their elbows
- Bandanna: Often seen hanging out of a dancer's back pocket, wrapped around the wrist or the head
- Sneakers: The brand, color, and style are all important.

▲ Hip-hop artist Missy Elliott has developed her own clothing label with a famous sportswear brand.

Promoting brands

In the 1980s, fashion and hip-hop combined, as many sports brands used hip-hop artists to promote their clothing and footwear. Hip-hop artists Run DMC were often seen wearing the striped tracksuits of a famous sports brand. In recent years, other hip-hop artists have developed their own clothing labels, including Sean "P. Diddy" Combs and Jay-Z's Rocawear. Russell Simmons, who launched Def Jam Records, also launched the successful clothing brand Phat Farm in 1993.

Other hip-hop artists, such as female rap icon Missy Elliott, have also been used to promote brands of sportswear. More recently, b-boys and b-girls have been advertising hair products and cars.

URBAN DANCE IN COMMERCE

Urban dance can now be seen in music videos, movies, and even in computer games. Over the last several years, its popularity has grown massively, due to the stars who are dancing it and the products that are made to sell it.

Music videos

In music videos, dance movement is set to a music track by the artist or **choreographer**. Some pop artists dance in their own videos, while others hire dancers to star alongside them. One of the most respected artists and dancers is Michael Jackson.

Michael Jackson is thought by many to be one of the most natural, stunning, and inspirational dancers of all time. He has helped to popularize dance styles such as the moonwalk. In his 1983 video "Thriller," Jackson and his dancers perform a variety of street dance styles that show **popping** and **locking** influences. The dancing in the video is slick, exciting, and involves intricate routines. "Thriller" was the most influential music video of its time. It rewrote the rules and opened up endless possibilites for the music video.

More recently, a range of music stars, including Usher, Missy Elliott, and the Black Eyed Peas, have used elements of different street dance styles in their music videos.

Amazing fact

"Thriller"
Michael Jackson's "Thriller" video was 14 minutes long. It contained body popping and street dance styles. At the time it was the most expensive music video ever made, costing about $1 million. The "Thriller" album sold more than 50 million copies worldwide—more than any other album before it.

Movies

One of the first movies to take on urban dance and hip-hop culture was *Style Wars*, which was made in 1983. This documentary focused on the emerging hip-hop scene in New York. Other dance documentary films followed.

In the last several years many movies have been made that revolve around this subject. A recent break dance documentary is *Planet B-Boy* (2007), which looks at b-boys today. It follows five **crews** leading up to and taking part in the Battle of the Year competition in Germany.

Computer games

In 2006 *B-Boy*, the first ever computerized b-boy game, was launched. Players can battle, pick characters, and try dance combos at a series of different events. It also features some classic funk and hip-hop tracks to dance to.

◀ Michael Jackson performs his moves on stage in 1984. Jackson made the moonwalk famous and inspired many dancers with his sensational routines.

HIP-HOP AND CHOREOGRAPHY

When hip-hop dance is performed, it can be both **choreographed** and **improvised**. This is different from most other styles of dance, which are normally entirely choreographed. There are many different areas in which choreography is used. These include music videos, **b-boying** competitions, hip-hop theater, and when hip-hop is mixed with other dance forms.

▼ Known for her amazing dance skills, Madonna and her dancers perform on stage in 2007.

Music videos and tours

As a recording artist, there is a huge amount of money to be made if your music video gains mass appreciation or if your tour sells out. Finding the hottest **choreographer** to create the **freshest** dance moves, routines, and stunning visuals has become essential in the fight to sell records.

Jamie King

In the last 10 years, there has been one major force behind some of the most unique and explosive music videos and tours. Jamie King is now recognized as one of the most innovative directors and choreographers working in the music industry today. Born in Verona, Wisconsin, King studied dance at the West Side Performing Arts Studio in Madison, Wisconsin, before gaining a scholarship to the Tremaine/Sleight Dance Studio in Los Angeles. In 1993 King worked for the music star Prince, who taught him about the fusion of music and movement, as well as staging and lighting. In 1995 King won an Emmy Award nomination for his work on the American Music Awards. He then worked for Salt-N-Pepa, En Vogue, Michael Jackson, Smashing Pumpkins, Britney Spears, Ricky Martin, and many others, before building a long partnership with Madonna.

King worked alongside Madonna from 1996 to 2006 to create the ideas for her videos and world tour. For this he picked up an MTV Award nomination and was catapulted into the spotlight. King uses urban dance styles in his choreography. He takes the story of the music as a starting point, then creates his routines. For Madonna's world tour she was accompanied by a **crew** of top break dancers.

In 2005 King linked up with a famous sportswear brand to produce a workout DVD and fitness program that is now taught in gyms across the world. Using a variety of hip-hop moves, cardio, stretching, and other dance styles, the workout is a fusion of sports and dance.

Biography

Marty Kudelka

Marty Kudelka is a U.S. choreographer to the stars. Originally a b-boy, Marty soon became a teacher, setting up his own studios in Dallas, Texas. He crafted his skills there before moving to Los Angeles and establishing himself as a leading choreographer. Kudelka co-choreographed Janet Jackson's world tour "All For You" and worked with Pink and 'N SYNC. He went on to choreograph Justin Timberlake's music videos "Like I Love You," "Cry Me a River," "Rock Your Body," and "Señorita," which helped launch Timberlake's career as a solo artist.

▲ Music star and dancer Justin Timberlake holds a "**freeze**" as he performs in 2003.

B-BOY COMPETITIONS

The ultimate goal for any budding b-boy or b-girl is either to be crowned world champion or to win the world **crew** title. **B-boying** has always been about competing with your opponents for the best style and moves. Earning a place to compete in the world championships takes hours of practice and dedication. To be the ultimate winner requires an extra-special touch. Hundreds of competitions take place across the globe. Battles between solo b-boys or b-girls, crews, **lockers**, and **poppers** can take many forms.

The circle

In the early days, b-boys would start to dance, and onlookers would gather around in a circle. When they finished their moves, other b-boys watching would come into the circle and challenge them. Battles were born. The circle has remained an essential part of b-boying, and battles take place all over the world.

▼ Korean b-boys perform at the Battle of the Year in 2004. Known for their power moves, fluidity, and dynamic precision, Korean b-boys are the world b-boy champions.

▲ These Chinese b-boys
are midway through a
head spin.

Battles

Battles between b-boys or b-girls and crew battles are sometimes judged by the crowd watching and sometimes by a panel of experts. Different battles have different rules, but generally b-boys are judged on style, **top rock**, footwork, **freezes**, and power. Other factors are innovation (new ideas), knowledge, and execution (how a dancer carries out a move or series of moves).

Crew battles are normally made up of up to eight b-boys or b-girls from a crew. The battles often involve aspects of **choreographed** routines using partner work, acrobatics, power, and combinations. These can be judged on synchronicity (performing moves exactly together), difficulty, stage presence (projecting confidence), and use of music. B-boys and b-girls always choreograph their own material for a battle, because the moves and routines they produce represent their crew and style.

From flexibility and strength to agility and acrobatics, b-boying can only be described as daring, explosive, athletic, skilled, and powerful. With b-boys trying to outdo each other by discovering the next new move or by adding just one more spin, the art of b-boying will constantly develop.

HIP-HOP THEATER

Hip-hop theater uses the traditional elements of theater, such as performing on a stage using lighting, sets, and costumes, but it also adds the four elements of hip-hop: **DJ-ing**, **MC-ing**, **graffiti**, and **b-boying**. Most performances will involve a theme or narrative, sometimes surrounding a character involved in hip-hop. When a dance company performs hip-hop theater, it is normally known as a hip-hop dance theater company.

Rennie Harris

The main name in U.S. hip-hop theater is Rennie Harris, a highly acclaimed **choreographer**. Growing up in Philadelphia, Harris was heavily involved in the early hip-hop scene, dancing with Step Masters, the Scanner Boys, and Magnificent Force. He has taught workshops at many world-class universities and dance centers, including UCLA (University of California at Los Angeles), Columbia College in Chicago, and the Broadway Dance Center in New York.

▼ Dancers from Rennie Harris's production of *Students of the Asphalt Jungle* perform their footwork.

Harris formed the company Pure Movement and has created many pieces of hip-hop theater, including *Lorenzo's Oil*, *Facing Mekka*, and *Rome & Jewels*, which premiered in 2000. *Rome & Jewels* uses b-boying, **popping**, **locking**, and other street dance forms in a dramatic and athletic re-telling of the classic Shakespeare tale *Romeo and Juliet*. It is the longest-touring hip-hop dance theater work in U.S. history, and it continues to impress audiences around the world today.

Jonzi D

In the United Kingdom, Jonzi D is a leading figure in hip-hop dance theater, at the cutting edge of current developments. He learned to dance in the 1980s, and his influences were the Rock Steady **Crew**, Poppin Pete, and Poppin Tacho from *Breakdance*: *The Movie*. He trained at the London School of Contemporary Dance, and in 1995 he created Lyrikal Fearta. When Jonzi first started creating his work, he felt that he was the only person doing this style. He said: "To me it completely made sense to use break dance and popping as a way of finding new movement."

▶ Jonzi D is a pioneer of hip-hop theater and the director of Breakin Convention.

Jonzi D has worked with many dance companies, including Benji Reid (see box), Robert Hylton, and ACE Dance and Music. He works with other dance styles in addition to hip-hop. He says that when he creates work he starts from a theme, usually taken from the **lyrics:** "I don't **choreograph.** I **devise** and direct. I then bring in choreographers that suit the overall theme. I am a ChoreoPoet."

He has helped to create fashion shows including *40 degrees* (2006) and *State Property* for Rocawear. Jonzi is also an MC and a poet, and he has worked with many artists, including Mannafest and Gangstarr. Currently, he runs Jonzi D Productions, which is an associate company of Sadler's Wells Theater in London, England.

▼ Dancers perform Jonzi D's latest work, *TAG . . . Me vs. the City*. The show explores the idea of using the body to create words (known as "physical calligraphy").

Jonzi D believes that hip-hop theater is about creating dramatic performances using the styles, techniques, and values that come from hip-hop culture: "It is important to remember the roots of hip-hop and that this dance style grew out of a group of kids expressing themselves, going to clubs and battling."

Today, his influences are Frank II Louise (France), Project Soul (Korea), and Kennrick (United Kingdom) from urban dance group Boy Blue.

Biography

Benji Reid

Benji Reid's influences when growing up were Jeffy Daniels, Michael Jackson, and Raymond Campbell. In 1986 he was the European Body Popping Champion, and he came second in the World Dance Championships. He trained at the Northern School of Contemporary Dance in Leeds, England. He has made a name for himself as a dancer, actor, creative producer, and director. In 1996 he codirected *Aeroplane Man* with Jonzi D and later toured *Paper Jackets*. He has since produced and directed many shows, including his latest work, *Life of a B-Boy*. This piece of hip-hop theater uses break dance, text, and live DJ-ing. Benji now runs the Breaking Cycles theater group, which is a national and international voice for hip-hop theater. It plays a key role in the development of hip-hop theater as an art form.

HIP-HOP AND THE DANCE WORLD

Hip-hop has influenced many different areas of the dance world today.

Contemporary dance

With contemporary dance companies striving to be the most innovative, to work with the hippest **choreographers**, and to sell tickets to an ever-changing audience, contemporary dance has had to make changes. With hip-hop dance attracting big audiences, contemporary dance has found a new competitor. Changing its image into one that is hip, fashionable, and cutting edge is something that is increasingly important.

In the performances of many modern dance companies, hip-hop moves including **freezes**, footwork, and acrobatics can clearly be seen, but mixed in with more balletic and contemporary styles. In the pieces *Infinity* by Australian choreographer Garry Stewart and *Anatomica #3* by Canadian choreographer André Gingras, there are influences from gymnastics, yoga, break dance, and even what seems to be a giant skateboard ramp, from which dancers jump, dive, and fall. Choreographer Rafael Bonachela has also created works influenced by hip-hop and pop.

Influenced by hip-hop dance, the Rambert Dance Company performs Australian choreographer Garry Stewart's *Infinity* in 2007.

Dancer Bill Shannon has been on crutches since he was a boy. Over time he has created an acrobatic, unique style of dancing that utilizes his crutches. He developed this style on the streets, and today, performing for large audiences, he incorporates DJs and hip-hop movement into his work.

Modern ballet

In modern ballets, there is also the influence of hip-hop. As traditional ballet companies have produced more modern ballet, and modern ballet companies renamed themselves contemporary dance companies, it was not going to be long before the worlds of hip-hop and ballet merged.

The Pacific Northwest Ballet from Seattle, Washington, is a traditional ballet company producing classics such as *Swan Lake*, *The Nutcracker*, and *Giselle*, yet it is also producing modern ballets. In 2006 it engaged the choreographer Victor Quijada to create a new work. A former b-boy and dancer with Twyla Tharp Dance, Quijada created a work called *Suspension of Disbelief*, which is a unique mixture of break dance and ballet. For him the two styles work well together, as the refined is mixed with the **raw**. *Suspension of Disbelief* won critical acclaim.

The partnership between hip-hop dance and choreography is developing all the time. From the explosive routines in the b-boy competition to slick, synchronized music videos, from **devised** hip-hop theater to the fusion of the classical and urban styles, hip-hop dance is still being explored.

TRAINING FOR URBAN DANCE

There are many opportunities for the urban dancer these days, either in the commercial world or in the theater. Urban dancers can dance in music videos, perform with a dance company, or enter **b-boying** competitions.

▲ These students in a hip-hop class are learning an **up rock**, one of the basics of break dance.

Formal training

Formal dance training is studying dance at a practical level in preparation for a career in dance. This normally takes place at a dance school or a college.

Many dance schools offer courses that cover some elements of urban dance such as **locking**, house dance, or street jazz. The training is very competitive, so to get a place at one of these schools you generally need to have previous dance experience and a flair for performance.

From the street

As urban dance styles flood onto our TV screens, more and more young people are learning the latest moves directly from movies or music videos. Some of the best urban dancers working today have taught themselves, rather than trained in a traditional way. This is not always easy. You have to be very motivated. You can decide to attend regular classes at a local dance center. This is always a good idea because you may get to work with amazing teachers and also find new inspirations.

▲ A crowd looks on as a b-boy dances on the streets. This b-boy is halfway through a power move called a **windmill**.

If you want to become a b-boy or b-girl and enter competitions, training is a very different story. Although dance centers may offer break dance classes, some b-boys would say learning in this way goes against the origins of the dance style. The style and individuality of the moves are best learned in an informal setting.

Some hip-hop theater and dance companies are looking for dancers with a wide range of skills who can b-boy as well as do ballet or contemporary dance. Formal dance training may then be necessary.

How to train

The type of training you choose is a personal decision and can depend on what career you would like in the future—dancer, **choreographer**, teacher, or b-boy/b-girl. It is always important to get advice if you are not sure.

NEW DIRECTIONS FOR HIP-HOP

In 2004 Jonzi D brought hip-hop to the masses with a festival of hip-hop called Breakin Convention. It has continued every year since. With companies from the United States (Electric Boogaloos), the United Kingdom (Boy Blue), and Europe (Frank II Louise) performing, the dance world stood up and began to take notice. Theatrical displays from some of the world's legendary hip-hop artists, as well as from emerging talent, took hip-hop to a new level.

In 2006 Benji Reid's Breaking Cycles ran Process 06, two weeks of discovery and development for the next generation of **hip-hop headz** led by some of the leading hip-hop practitioners in dance, theater, and music.

Hip-hop is everywhere today. Leading artists and companies working in the field of hip-hop dance are Jonzi D, Funk Stylerz, Robert Hylton and his company Urban Classicism, Freshmess, 2FaCeD DaNcE Company, and Mickael Marso Riverie's Company Decalage. Hip-hop influences are also apparent in the work of dance companies such as Alvin Ailey American Dance Theater, Hubbard Street Dance, and Bill T. Jones/Arnie Zane Dance Company.

Urban dance shows now regularly go on tour. With conferences for b-boys, break dance moves in dance exams, and the influence of hip-hop in other art forms, what paths will hip-hop dance now take? In the future hip-hop or urban dance will surely involve

Dance facts

Hip-hop awards

The BET Hip Hop Awards are hosted by Black Entertainment Television every year. Categories such as best hip-hop video and best hip-hop dance of the year allow hip-hop achievements to receive recognition. More long-standing awards are also acknowledging hip-hop. The Bessie Awards honored Bill T. Jones/Arnie Zane Dance Company and their collaborators for exceptional achievements in choreography, for their performance of *Chapel/Chapter* at **Harlem** Stage.

new fusions with other creative forms. As it picks up pace and gains a reputation for being exciting and explosive, what we can certainly say is that hip-hop is on the move.

"The future is acknowledging global and regional development in hip-hop dance. The best new ideas have always come from the street in music and dance. The effect this has had on the dance world throughout history is obvious. Once jazz dance was a street form. Now it is a staple of musical theater and taught in theater schools. The future of hip-hop is therefore inevitable."

Jonzi D

▼ The Alvin Ailey American Dance Theater performs *Firebird* in 2007.

TIMELINE

Hip-hop dance is currently one of the world's fastest-growing types of dance and industry. Here is a summary of its short history.

1925 "Snake Hips" Earl Tucker performs moves that later inspire **b-boying**.

1960s: Small beginnings
The civil rights movement emerges in the United States. The unrest felt in society is mirrored culturally. Out of the **Bronx** comes a new subculture: hip-hop.

1966 Political **graffiti** begins to appear across cities in the United States, gaining the attention of the press and public.

1969 Afrika Bambaattaa forms Universal Zulu Nation.

First wave of b-boys.
Don Campbell invents the funk dance style **locking**.

1970s: B-boying finds its feet
The world of b-boying takes off.

1971 *The New York Times* publishes an article on graffiti artist Taki 183.

TV program *Soul Train* starts, featuring the Lockers.
James Brown releases "Get on the Good Foot."

1974 Universal Zulu Nation is re-named Zulu Nation.
Second wave of b-boys.

1977 Third wave of b-boys.
The Rock Steady **Crew** is formed.
Electric Boogaloo Lockers is formed.

1979 Sugarhill Gang releases the single "Rapper's Delight."

1980s: Break dance and the media
B-boying is called break dance, the media discovers hip-hop, and rap develops its first female stars.

1981 The Dynamic Rockers and the Rock Steady Crew battle at the Lincoln Center, New York.

1982 The Rock Steady Crew performs at the Ritz nightclub, New York.

1983 The Rock Steady Crew releases the single "Hey You, The Rock Steady Crew."
The documentary *Style Wars*, exploring New York's graffiti scene, is first shown on TV.

Rapper Ice T releases his first single.
The Rock Steady Crew make a guest appearance in the movie *Flashdance*.

Run DMC release the iconic single "It's Like That."
Michael Jackson first performs the moonwalk on the Motown 25 TV special and his "Thriller" video is released.
The Fat Boys (Darren "Buffy" Robinson, Doug E. Fresh, and Biz Markie) win a talent competition at Radio City Hall, in New York, sparking the first wave of **beatboxers**.

1985 Female rappers Salt-N-Pepa burst onto the music scene.

1986 Benji Reid becomes European body **popping** champion.

1990s: Clowning, krumping, beatboxing, and clothing
Hip-hop finds new areas of influence.

1990 The first annual b-boy battle, International Breakdance Cup, is launched.

1991 Mr. Wiggles from Electric Boogaloos and some members of the Rock Steady Crew produce the first hip-hop musical, *So What Happens Now?*

1992 Tommy the Clown makes his mark on the hip-hop scene by introducing it to **krumping**.

1993 Clothing label Phat Farm is formed.

1994 The first B-Boy Summit is held in San Diego, California.

1995 Jonzi D creates Lyrikal Fearta.

1996 Benji Reid and Jonzi D direct the movie *Aeroplane Man*.

1999 Rahzel (also known as "The Noise") releases one of the most influential beatboxing albums of all time.

2000s: A new era for hip-hop dance
Hip-hop dance theater storms onto stages, Korea battles its way to the top of the b-boy league, and b-boying takes on its history with conferences and workshops.

2000 Rennie Harris premieres *Rome & Jewels* with his company Pure Movement.

2001 Korea explodes onto the b-boy scene.

2002 The movie *The Freshest Kids—History of a B-Boy* is released.
Crazy Legs of the Rock Steady Crew is inducted into the Hip-Hop Hall of Fame.

2004 The first festival dedicated to hip-hop dance, Breakin Convention, takes place at Sadlers Wells, in London, England.

2005 The documentary movie *Rize* is created by director David La Chapelle and later released.
Director/**choreographer** Jamie King releases a hip-hop workout video.

2006 Skeeter Rabbit, a former member of the Electric Boogaloos, dies.
The first b-boy computer game is released.
Suspension of Disbelief, created by Victor Quijada, wins critical acclaim.
Benji Reid's theater group Breaking Cycles runs "Process 06" for emerging **hip-hop headz**.

2007 The documentary movie *Planet B-Boy* is released.
The Rock Steady Crew's 30th anniversary.

GLOSSARY

b-boying (also called "break dancing") athletic, stylized, and fast-paced form of dance in which dancers (b-boys or b-girls) often perform and compete

beatboxing (also called "vocal percussion") art of producing drum sounds, musical sounds, singing, or scratching by using the mouth, lips, tongue, voice, and teeth

break instrumental or percussion section in a track of music

Bronx borough (region) of New York City on the mainland, often considered to be the home of hip-hop

choreograph make dances

choreographer person who makes dances

crew group of b-boys or b-girls

devise when a group of artists work together to develop an original theater or dance production. It is different from choreographing because it involves more than one person's ideas.

DJ-ing when a person plays records to entertain people in clubs or on the radio. "DJ" is short for "disc jockey."

down rock rhythmic weaving of legs and feet in a continuous circle low around the hand that carries the dancer's weight

drum 'n' bass type of electronic dance music in which the beat is normally between 160 and 180 beats per minute

flare (also known as a gym flare) break dance move in which dancers support themselves with their hands and rotates their legs around their body

floor rock old-style break dancing that took place entirely on the floor, involving fast-paced and complex footwork

freeze break dance move in which the dancer is completely still, or frozen, normally balancing on a body part, such as the hands, elbow, or head and shoulders

fresh looking good

graffiti art of spraying, painting, or drawing images or names

Harlem neighborhood in New York City, with a high percentage of African-American residents

head spin spinning headstand. A b-boy will often use his legs to either control or increase the number of spins.

hip-hop headz slang term for a person who is totally dedicated to hip-hop

homophobia fear of and prejudice against homosexuals

improvise make something up on the spot

krumping energetic form of street dance involving large upper-body movements

locking style of street dance that features strong arm and hand movements with relaxed hips

lyrics words that are set to music

MC-ing when a person speaks, freestyles, or performs to an audience to keep a party or performance going. "MC" is short for "Master of Ceremonies."

popping funk and street style of dance in which the dancer contracts and releases the muscles

raw untrained and natural

scratching art of moving a record back and forth under the needle in a rhythmic fashion. It used in turntablism and also copied in beatboxing (vocal scratching).

street entrepreneurship create something out of nothing—people who organize or promote a business from the streets

street knowledge news and issues of a community passed on from one generation to the next through talking

top rock upright movements performed at the beginning of a break dance set

turntablism musical art form that involves changing the sounds produced by records using turntables and a mixer

up rock dancing "battle" in which the dancers are very close but do not actually touch

windmill core of most power moves—a back spin and hand glide freeze combined

worm move done either forward or backward by shifting the weight from the upper body to the lower body, creating a rippling motion

FURTHER INFORMATION

Books

Baker, Soreen. *The History of Rap and Hip-Hop*. Farmington Hills, Mich.: Lucent, 2006.

Shapiro, Peter. *The Rough Guide to Hip-Hop*. New York: Rough Guides, 2005.

Slavicek, Louise Chipley. *Hip-Hop Stars: Run DMC*. New York: Chelsea House, 2007.

Websites

If you want to discover more about hip-hop dance, check out these websites.

www.bboyworld.com

The website for all things b-boy. See also "bboy tube" from this website. Features breaking and beatboxing videos.

www.hiphop-network.com

The Hip-Hop Network provides videos, recordings, games, and more.

www.battleoftheyear.de

The website for the b-boying Battle of the Year.

www.urbanfreeflow.com

The website for all things related to parkour and free running.

INDEX